HSC
Health & Safety Commission

Commercial diving projects offshore

Diving at Work Regulations 1997

APPROVED CODE
OF PRACTICE

L103

HSE BOOKS

The Approved Code of Practice

This Approved Code of Practice has been approved by the Health and Safety Commission with the consent of the Secretary of State. It gives practical advice on how to comply with the law. If you follow the advice you will be doing enough to comply with the law in respect of those specific matters on which the Approved Code of Practice gives advice. You may use alternative methods to those set out in the Approved Code of Practice in order to comply with the law.

However, the Approved Code of Practice has a special legal status. If you are prosecuted for breach of health and safety law, and it is proved that you did not follow the relevant provisions of the Approved Code of Practice, you will need to show that you have complied with the law in some other way or a court will find you at fault.

Contents

By virtue of section 16(1) of the Health and Safety at Work etc Act 1974, and with the consent of the Secretary of State for Environment, Transport and the Regions, the Health and Safety Commission has on 10 December 1997 approved the Code of Practice entitled *Commercial diving projects offshore*.

The Code of Practice is approved for the purposes of providing practical guidance with respect to the requirements of the Diving at Work Regulations 1997 (SI 1997 No 2776) and with respect to regulation 3 of the Management of Health and Safety at Work Regulations 1992 (SI 1992 No 2051). The Code of Practice comes into force on 1 April 1998.

Reference in this Code of Practice to another document does not imply approval by HSC of that document except to the extent necessary to give effect to this Code of Practice.

Signed

ROSEMARY BANNER
Secretary to the Health and Safety Commission

19 January 1998

This publication contains the Approved Code of Practice (ACOP) and additional guidance for commercial diving projects offshore, together with the relevant regulations from the Diving at Work Regulations 1997. The full text of the Regulations (SI 1997 No 2776) is available from the Stationery Office.

For convenience, the text of the Regulations is included in *italic* type, with the accompanying ACOP in **bold** type.

Explanation and intention of the Approved Code of Practice

1   This Approved Code of Practice (ACOP) (referred to as the Code) gives advice on meeting the requirements of the Diving at Work Regulations 1997 (referred to as the Diving Regulations) for commercial diving projects offshore. In particular, the Code gives advice on how to comply with those Regulations that are set out in general terms.

2   It should not be assumed that compliance with the Diving Regulations means that all aspects of the law are being complied with. The requirements of other legislation may also need to be fulfilled. A list of other major health and safety at work legislation in force when this Code was published is set out in Annex 4.

Health and safety legislation

3   The basis of health and safety law in Great Britain is the Health and Safety at Work etc Act 1974 (the HSW Act). The HSW Act sets out the general duties that employers and the self-employed have towards employees and members of the public, and the duties that employees have to themselves and to each other. These duties are qualified in the HSW Act by the principle of *so far as is reasonably practicable.*

4   Health and safety regulations are law, approved by Parliament. These are usually made under the HSW Act following proposals from the Health and Safety Commission (HSC). Regulations set out requirements which must be met.

Scope and areas covered by the Code

5   This Code applies to all diving projects:

(a)   at sea outside the United Kingdom territorial waters adjacent to Great Britain (generally 12 nautical miles from the low water line) which are covered by the Health and Safety at Work etc Act 1974 (Application outside Great Britain) Order 1995. This will include all diving operations in UK designated areas of the continental shelf undertaken in connection with offshore installations, wells and pipeline works, and with those parts of mines which extend outside the 12-mile limit;

(b)   at sea off or in connection with offshore installations and pipeline works within the 12-mile limit;

(c)   where closed bell* or saturation diving techniques† are used (both offshore and inshore);

(d)   where diving takes place from vessels maintaining station by the use of dynamic positioning;

(e)   for all dives below 50 metres except for those diving projects covered by the following Codes:

---

*A diving bell is a submersible compression chamber used for transferring divers under pressure to and from the worksite.

†Saturation diving is the diving technique used during diving operations where the diver has reached the full saturation state for the pressure and breathing mixture being used. When this state has been reached the time required for decompression is not further increased in relation to the duration of the dive.

(i)   Media diving projects;

(ii)   Recreational diving projects;

(iii)   Scientific and archaeological diving projects.

Who wrote the Code and how it was agreed

6   A working party of representatives from the International Marine Contractors Association (IMCA) worked with the Health and Safety Executive (HSE) to produce a draft Code that was published by HSC in July 1996 for public consultation.

Updating arrangements

7   There will be regular discussions between HSE, IMCA and other parties in the industry to discuss the current applicability of this Code. When technology, industry standards or practices change, consideration will be given to amending this Code. All amendments will be the subject of formal public consultation.

The other diving Codes

8   There are four other Codes that cover diving at work:

(a)   Commercial diving projects inland/inshore (ISBN 0 7176 1495 6);

(b)   Media diving projects (ISBN 0 7176 1497 2);

(c)   Recreational diving projects (ISBN 0 7176 1496 4);

(d)   Scientific and archaeological diving projects (ISBN 0 7176 1498 0).

9   Each of these Codes has been drafted by HSE with the help of the industry associations for the relevant sector and covers standards and practices that are relevant to that sector's particular area of diving.

Sources of information

10   The Codes do not cover the detailed technical aspects of controlling the risks from diving at work. Separate, non-statutory guidance published by HSC provides detailed technical advice on assessing and minimising the risks. Guidance is also published by IMCA (and its predecessor the Association of Offshore Diving Contractors (AODC)) and the Diving Medical Advisory Committee (DMAC). A list of this guidance is set out in Annex 5. You should check that the list is still current.

11   When an ACOP paragraph has an adjacent asterisk $(^\star)$ this indicates that relevant industry technical guidance is listed in Annex 5. This does not mean, however, that the industry guidance has the legal status of an Approved Code of Practice.

Definitions in the Regulations

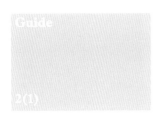

(1) "diver" means a person at work who dives;

12 The phrase 'at work' means as an employee or as a self-employed person. The phrase covers divers who dive as part of their duties as an employee and divers who are in business on their own account during the time that they devote themselves to work as a self-employed diver. Diving does not have to be the main work activity of the employee or the self-employed person. The Diving Regulations apply when at least one diver is at work.

(2) For the purposes of these Regulations a person "dives" if -

(a) he enters -

(i)   water or any other liquid; or

(ii)   a chamber in which he is subject to pressure greater than 100 millibars above atmospheric pressure; and

(b) in order to survive in such an environment he breathes in air or other gas at a pressure greater than atmospheric pressure;

13 Environments such as scientific clean rooms or submersible craft subjected to an internal pressure of less than 100 millibars above atmospheric pressure are not covered by the Diving Regulations.

(1) "diving project" means any activity, made up of one or more diving operations, in which at least one person takes part or will take part as a diver and extends from the time when that person, or the first such person, commences to prepare to dive until that person, or the last such person, has left the water, chamber or other environment in which the dive, or any part of the dive, took place and has completed any requisite decompression procedures, including, where it may be reasonably anticipated that this will be needed, any therapeutic recompression;

14 A 'diving project' is the term used for the overall diving job - whether it lasts two hours or two months.

15 Diving project can apply to both a continuous period of elevated pressure, as in saturation diving, and to a number of diving operations, possibly taking place over several days, where the divers are not under continuous elevated pressure.

16 The diving project does not necessarily finish once the last diver has returned to atmospheric pressure. Most decompression procedures require the diver to remain in the close vicinity of a recompression chamber for a specified time in case there is a need for treatment of symptoms of decompression illness. The diving project is only completed once that time period has expired.

Regulation 8

Regulation
2(1)

(1)   "diving operation" means a diving operation identified in the diving project plan pursuant to regulation 8(3);

Regulation

8(3)

(3)   The diving project plan shall identify each diving operation which makes up the diving project and the nature and size of any diving operation so identified shall be such that it can be safely supervised by one person.

Guide

17   Diving operations can be made up of either a number of dives or even a single dive. A diving operation is the portion of a diving project identified in the diving project plan which can be supervised safely by one person. It will normally be evident what this portion of work is, but factors such as the task, site conditions and the diving techniques to be used, all contribute to making the decision. For example, a 28-day diving project may be made up of 40 diving operations.

18   The diving contractor has the main responsibility, under the Diving Regulations, for ensuring that a safe diving project is carried out. The diving contractor must determine, after studying the risk assessment, how many diving operations the diving project is to be broken down into and must appoint a supervisor to supervise each operation. The diving contractor has responsibility for ensuring that all parts of a diving project are managed in such a way as to ensure the safety of the people involved in it. If there is more than one diving operation being conducted at the same time, as part of the diving project, the diving contractor has a responsibility to ensure that there is proper co-ordination.

19   The supervisor has a duty to direct the diving operation safely. If a supervisor does not agree with the size or complexity of the portion of the diving project allocated as his or her operation to supervise, the supervisor should raise the matter with the diving contractor. A supervisor should not participate in a diving operation that he or she considers to be unsafe because, for example, in the supervisor's opinion it is too large for one person to supervise safely or that the supervisor knows that he or she is not competent to supervise.

2(1), 8(3)

Regulation 2

Regulation

2(1)

(1)   "the 1995 Order" means the Health and Safety at Work etc. Act 1974 (Application outside Great Britain) Order 1995[a];

(a) SI 1995/263

Regulation 3

Regulation

3(2)

(2)   These Regulations shall apply to and in relation to the premises and activities outside Great Britain to which sections 1 to 59 and 80 to 82 of the Health and Safety at Work etc. Act 1974 apply by virtue of the 1995 order as they apply within Great Britain.

20

The Diving Regulations cover all diving projects in Great Britain, within territorial waters as well as oil- and gas-related diving projects (including diving projects involving offshore installations and any preparatory work and pipelines) beyond territorial waters on the UK designated areas of the continental shelf.

(1) These Regulations shall apply to and in relation to any diving project apart from the following -

(a) the care or treatment of patients in a hospital or other place, not under the control of the diving contractor, where emergency medical treatment is provided or in transit to such hospital or place where the means of transit is provided by or in respect of the hospital or other place;

21   The use of hyperbaric chambers within diving projects is covered by the Diving Regulations. However, those receiving hyperbaric treatment at a hospital or other place are outside the scope of the Diving Regulations. This is to avoid duplication of responsibilities when another authority is involved in the medical treatment of a diver.

22   Where hyperbaric treatment is to be provided in a compression chamber provided by a person other than the diving contractor for that diving project, the arrangements for this should be covered in the diving project plan. The Diving Regulations do not apply to the hyperbaric treatment provided by that other person.

(1) These Regulations shall apply to and in relation to any diving project apart from the following -

(c) work carried out in any air which is compressed in order to prevent the ingress of ground water to the works or to stabilise the area around the works.

23   Construction activities that are subject to the Compressed Air Regulations 1996 where the primary purpose is either to keep ground water out or to make a structure stable are not covered by the Diving Regulations.

Regulation 5

(1) No person at work shall dive in a diving project and no employer shall employ any person in such a project unless there is one person and one person only who is the diving contractor for that project.

24   The term 'person' used to identify the diving contractor under this regulation means a person with legal identity such as an individual or a company and includes a body of people corporate or incorporate.

Clients and others

Every person who to any extent is responsible for, has control over or is engaged in a diving project or whose acts or omissions could adversely affect the health and safety of persons engaged in such a project, shall take such measures as it is reasonable for a person in his position to take to ensure that these Regulations are complied with.

25   The actions and activities of other people can affect the safety of the dive team even though they are not members of the team, and therefore they may have responsibilities for ensuring that the Regulations are complied with for matters under their control. These people include:

(a)   the client who has placed a contract with a diving contractor to deliver a diving project. The client will usually be the operator or owner of a proposed or existing installation or pipeline where diving work is going to take place, or a contractor acting on behalf of the operator or owner. If the operator or owner appoints an on-site representative, he or she must ensure that such a person is competent for the task;

(b)   the principal contractor carrying out work for the client and overseeing the work of the diving contractor;

(c)   the manager of an offshore installation from or near which a diving project is carried out;

(d)   a consultant acting for the client, operator, owner, or contractor;

(e)   a master of a vessel or floating structure from which diving is to take place, who controls the vessel or floating structure and who has overall responsibility for the safety of the vessel or floating structure and all personnel on it;

(f)   a superintendent, or other similar person, provided by the diving contractor may or may not be a member of the dive team, but nevertheless has a responsibility to ensure that the diving project is conducted safely because he or she is in overall control of the project. Such a person must be competent for the task. (See paragraph 91 for more information about superintendents.)

26   These people listed in paragraph 25 must consider carefully the actions required of them to comply with the Diving Regulations. They should, where appropriate:

(a)   take reasonable steps to ensure that any diving contractor selected is capable of complying with the Diving Regulations;

(b)   make available to the diving contractor the results of any risk assessments undertaken by other persons under other statutory legislation that could affect the health and safety of the dive team;

(c)   agree to provide facilities and extend all reasonable support to the supervisor or diving contractor in the event of an emergency. The diving project plan should reflect this;

(d)   consider whether any known underwater or above-water items of plant under their control may cause a hazard to the dive team.

Such items may include ship propellers, water intakes or discharge points causing suction or turbulence, gas flare mechanisms that may activate without warning, or plant liable to start operating automatically. The diving contractor should be informed of the location and nature of such hazards. This information should be provided in sufficient time so that it can be taken into account by the diving contractor when preparing the risk assessment before producing the diving project plan. They should also provide the diving contractor, in good time, with details of any changes to this information occurring before or during the course of the diving project;

(e)   ensure that suitable facilities and time are available to the diving contractor to allow for a familiarisation programme;

(f)   consider whether other activities in the vicinity affect the safety of the diving project, for example they may need to arrange for the suspension of loading or unloading of vessels, seismic operations, scaffolding work or similar activities;

(g)   ensure that they have a formal control system in place to cover diving activities, for example a permit-to-work system;

(h)   provide the diving contractor with details of any possible substance likely to be encountered by the dive team that would be a hazard to their health, for example drill cuttings on the seabed. This information must be provided in writing and in sufficient time to allow the diving contractor to carry out the relevant risk assessment and, if necessary, to take appropriate action;

(i)   keep the supervisor informed of any changes that may affect the supervisor's diving operation, for example vessel movement, so that diving can be suspended if the diving site is, or may be, endangered.

27   When diving from a dynamically positioned (DP) vessel, the responsible person on the DP control panel should inform the supervisor of any possible change in position-keeping ability as soon as it is known.

28   The duty under this regulation extends to diving contractors, supervisors, divers and people involved in the diving project whether directly or indirectly, for example crane operators and maintenance personnel. They should ensure that their tasks and how they undertake them do not affect the safety of the dive team.

4

Diving contractors

Regulation 5

(1)   No person at work shall dive in a diving project and no employer shall employ any person in such a project unless there is one person and one person only who is the diving contractor for that project.

(2)   The diving contractor shall, subject to paragraph (3), be the person who -

(a)   is the employer of the diver or divers engaged in the diving project; or

(b)   dives in the diving project as a self-employed diver.

(3)   Where there is more than one person falling within paragraph (2) those persons shall jointly appoint in writing before the commencement of the diving project one of themselves to act as diving contractor.

29   The Diving Regulations require that one person (see paragraph 24 for definition) is identified as the diving contractor for each diving project. The main duties under the Diving Regulations are placed on the diving contractor. The diving contractor will normally be the employer of the divers engaged in the diving project.

30   Where the client engages more than one employer of divers or more than one self-employed diver for the diving project, it must be established and recorded in writing who will be the designated diving contractor for that project.

31   The name of the diving contractor should be entered clearly on all diving project records. The name should also be notified in writing to the other personnel with responsibility for any location from or in the vicinity of which diving projects are carried out.

Regulation 6

(1)   The diving contractor shall ensure, so far as is reasonably practicable, that the diving project is planned, managed and conducted in a manner which protects the health and safety of all persons taking part in that project.

(3)   The diving contractor shall -

(d)   ensure, so far as reasonably practicable, that any person taking part in the diving project complies with the requirements and prohibitions imposed on him by or under the relevant statutory provisions and observes the provisions of the diving project plan;

(e)   ensure that a record containing the required particulars is kept for each diving operation.

32   The diving contractor's general responsibilities are to ensure that:

(a)   the diving project is properly and safely managed;

(b)   risk assessments have been carried out (see section 'Diving project plan and risk assessment');

(c)   the place from which the diving is to be carried out is suitable and safe;

(d)   a suitable diving project plan is prepared which includes emergency and contingency plans. The diving project plan should be authorised and dated by a responsible person acting on behalf of the diving contractor (see section 'Diving project plan and risk assessment');

(e)   the supervisor and dive team are fully briefed on the project and aware of the contents of the diving project plan;

(f)   there are sufficient personnel in the dive team to enable the diving project to be carried out safely (see section 'Dive teams and associated working practice');

(g)   the personnel are qualified and competent (see sections 'Supervisors' and 'Divers');

(h)   supervisors are appointed in writing and the extent of their control fully documented (see section 'Supervisors');

(i)   a suitable mobilisation and familiarisation programme is completed by all the members of the dive team. Other personnel involved in the diving project, for example ship's crew, may also need to complete the programme (see section 'Diving project plan and risk assessment');

(j)   adequate arrangements exist for first aid and medical treatment (see section 'Dive teams and associated working practice');

(k)   suitable and sufficient plant is provided and that it is correctly certified and maintained (see sections 'Diving plant' and 'Maintenance of diving plant');

(l)   the divers are medically fit to dive (see section 'Medical checks');

(m)   diving project records are kept containing the required details of the diving project (see Annex 1);

(n)   there is a clear reporting and responsibility structure laid down in writing; and

(o)   all other relevant Regulations are complied with.

Regulation 7

(1)   No person shall act as a diving contractor unless the particulars listed in Schedule 1 have been supplied in writing to the Executive by or in respect of that person.

(2)   Where there is a change in any of the particulars supplied under paragraph (1) the diving contractor shall ensure that details of the change are forthwith supplied in writing to the Executive.

33   Before any person (see paragraph 24 for definition) acts as a diving contractor he or she must ensure that HSE is provided with information on his or her identity and where he or she can be contacted. A diving contractor is also required to inform HSE of any subsequent changes to this information. Full details required are set out in Schedule 1 to the Diving Regulations. HSE will acknowledge receipt of such information.

Diving project plan and risk assessment

Regulation 6

Regulation

6(2)

(2) *The diving contractor shall -*

(a) *ensure that, before the commencement of the diving project, a diving project plan is prepared in respect of that project in accordance with regulation 8 and that the plan is thereafter updated as necessary during the continuance of the project;*

(b) *before the commencement of any diving operation -*

 (i) *appoint a person to supervise that operation in accordance with regulation 9;*

 (ii) *make a written record of that appointment; and*

 (iii) *ensure that the person appointed is supplied with a copy of any part of the diving project plan which relates to that operation;*

(c) *as soon as possible after the appointment of a supervisor, provide that supervisor with a written record of his appointment.*

Regulation 8

Regulation

8(1),(3)

(1) *The diving project plan shall be based on an assessment of the risks to the health and safety of any person taking part in the diving project and shall consist of a record of the outcome of the planning carried out in accordance with regulation 6(1) including all such information and instructions as are necessary to give advice to and to regulate the behaviour of those so taking part to ensure, so far as is reasonably practicable, their health and safety.*

(3) *The diving project plan shall identify each diving operation which makes up the diving project and the nature and size of any diving operation so identified shall be such that it can be safely supervised by one person.*

ACOP

34 **The diving contractor is responsible for ensuring that a risk assessment is carried out and a diving project plan prepared.**

Risk assessment

35 **A risk assessment must be carried out to identify site-specific hazards and their risks.**

36 **As a matter of safe working practice, the project risk assessment should be reviewed at regular intervals, even if the risk is minimal, to ensure that the risk assessment is still adequate and does not need to be revised.**

37 **A risk assessment made under the Diving Regulations will cover, in part, the obligation to make an assessment under the Management of Health and Safety at Work Regulations 1992. There will be no need to repeat those aspects of the assessment, so long as they remain valid, in any other assessment that is carried out. However, all significant risks not covered by the diving project assessment (including risks to members of the public arising from the diving project/diving activities)**

6(2), 8(1),(3)

must be covered by the risk assessment carried out under the Management of Health and Safety at Work Regulations 1992 or in any assessment required to be carried out under other specific regulations.

Diving project plan

38   Based on this information, the diving project plan must state how those hazards identified and risks assessed will be controlled. The diving project plan may include a diving contractor's standard operating rules, including generic risk assessments. All documents should show the date upon which they were prepared. The diving project plan should record the outcome of the planning carried out in preparing the risk assessment including all information and instructions which, so far as is reasonably practicable, are necessary to protect the health and safety of all those taking part in the diving project. It should also include procedures for conducting reviews of the site and updating the specific risk assessments.

39   The diving project plan must cover the general principles of the diving techniques to be used as well as the needs of the particular operation. It must also provide contingency procedures for any foreseeable emergency, including retrieving injured and unconscious divers from the water.

40   Each supervisor must be given a copy of that part of the diving project plan relevant to the diving operation that he or she will be supervising.

41   Some examples of hazards and risks are given in paragraphs 42-87. This is not a complete list of all hazards or all measures needed to control risk. In special circumstances, or if certain contingencies arise, more stringent safeguards may be needed.

General

Self-contained underwater breathing apparatus (SCUBA)

42[*]   SCUBA has inherent limitations and difficulties, such as limited breathing gas supplies, and is unsuitable for activities covered by this Code.

Use of compressed air or gas mixtures

43   Divers breathing a mixture of oxygen and nitrogen under pressure, whether compressed natural air or an artificial mixture, are at risk of both oxygen toxicity and nitrogen narcosis as the depth increases. The maximum depth for breathing mixtures of compressed air or oxygen and nitrogen is 50 metres of water. The recommended maximum partial pressure for oxygen is 1.5 atmosphere for surface-supplied diving equipment. This does not apply to therapeutic recompression.

Exposure limits for surface-orientated diving

44[*]   Diving carries an inherent risk of decompression illness (DCI). The incidence of DCI drops if the length of time that a diver spends at any particular depth is limited. The depth/time limitations are reproduced in Table 1. Use of this table has resulted in a significant reduction in the incidence of DCI, and dive plans should incorporate these maximum time limits.

* See Annex 5 for relevant technical guidance

45   When breathing oxy-nitrogen mixtures with oxygen percentages higher than in natural air, the equivalent air depth should be established. It is this equivalent air depth which should be used to establish bottom time limits.

46   Closed bell diving techniques should be used when diving deeper than 50 metres.

Table 1   Maximum bottom time limitations for surface decompression (SD), in-water decompression and transfer under pressure (TUP) decompression diving

Depth		Bottom time† limits (minutes)	
Metres	*Feet*	*TUP*	*SD and in water*
0-12	0-40	240	240
15	50	240	180
18	60	180	120
21	70	180	90
24	80	180	70
27	90	130	60
30	100	110	50
33	110	95	40
36	120	85	35
39	130	75	30
42	140	65	30
45	150	60	25
48	160	55	25
51	170	50	20

† Bottom time is the total elapsed time from when the diver is first exposed to a pressure greater than atmospheric, ie (a) when leaving the surface with an open device; (b) on the start of pressurisation when a closed device is employed in the observation mode, to the time (next whole minute) that the diver begins decompression (measured in minutes).

Water flow, intakes and discharges

47[*]   Divers are vulnerable to water flow, suction or turbulence - whether natural or caused by water intakes or discharges. If there are any intakes or discharges, suitable measures, for example mechanical isolation, should be taken to ensure that these cannot be operated while a diver is in the water unless the diver is protected by a suitable physical guard.

48   Measures to protect the diver should be part of a safe system of work, for example a permit-to-work system.

Restricted surface visibility

49[*]   Restricted surface visibility may affect the safety of the operation, for example when diving in darkness, heavy rain or fog. The diving project plan should identify when operations should be suspended because of restricted visibility.

[*] See Annex 5 for relevant technical guidance

Underwater currents

50[*] Currents may impose limitations on a diver's operational ability. Tide meters and tide tables may provide information on the current at different depths and can be used to help assess diving conditions.

Diving near remotely operated vehicle (ROV) operations

51[*] There are a number of safety considerations that should be taken into account when divers are working with, or in the vicinity of, ROVs. These include, for example, entanglement of umbilicals, physical contact and electrical hazards. Possible solutions include restricting umbilicals in length, employing guards and electrical trip mechanisms.

Safe use of electricity

52[*] Divers often come into contact with plant, including battery-powered equipment, operated by or carrying electricity. Battery-operated equipment used inside compression chambers can also be a hazard. Care should be taken to ensure that the divers and other members of the dive team are protected from the risk arising from the use of electricity, in particular from any shock hazard.

53[*] Recharging lead-acid batteries generates hydrogen which can present an explosion hazard in confined spaces. Care should be taken to provide adequate ventilation.

High-pressure water jetting

54[*] Even an apparently minor accident with this equipment has the potential to cause a serious internal injury to the diver. Safe operating procedures when using such equipment should be followed.

Lift bags

55[*] The use of lift bags under water can be hazardous, for example the uncontrolled ascent or descent of a load.

Abrasive cutting discs

56[*] The adhesive used in cutting discs tends to degrade under water causing the discs to break during use. Only dry discs not previously exposed to water should be used, and only those discs required for use by a diver at any one time should be taken under water.

Oxy-arc cutting and burning operations

57[*] There are dangers in the use of oxy-arc cutting and burning under water, for example explosions from trapped gases, and the trapping of a diver by items after cutting. Safe operating procedures should be followed.

Diving from dynamically positioned vessels

58[*] Diving from dynamically positioned vessels can be hazardous to divers because of the presence of rotating propellers and thrusters. Practical steps should be taken to prevent a diver or their umbilical coming into contact with a thruster or propeller.

6(2), 8(1),(3)

[*] See Annex 5 for relevant technical guidance

59[*] Any vessel operating on dynamic positioning should meet industry technical and operational standards.

Communications

60 In an emergency people tend to revert to their native language. If team members do not speak the same language this can cause an obvious risk. The diving project plan should state the language that is to be used during the diving project. All team members should be able to communicate clearly with each other at all times, particularly during emergencies.

Breathing gases

Quantity of gases

61[*] The quantities of gases required for diving operations, including primary, secondary and therapeutic treatments, should be calculated and procedures for the provision of them stated when planning a diving project. Allowances should be made for leakage, wastage, contingencies and so on. Diving should be stopped if the quantity of gas acceptable for safety purposes falls below an agreed minimum.

Quality of gases

62 Procedures for checking and maintaining gas purity standards should be provided.

Levels of oxygen in helium and nitrogen

63[*] Pure helium or nitrogen should not be used in diving operations except as a calibration gas or for a specific operational requirement. A small percentage of oxygen should be present in helium or nitrogen. The industry norm is 2%.

64[*] When an oxygen-helium or oxygen-nitrogen mixture is used as the diver-worn reserve supply it should contain a percentage of oxygen that allows it to be breathable over the largest possible depth range.

Contents of gas mixes

65[*] Breathing gases coming from suppliers will be colour-coded in accordance with international, European or national standards, and will be accompanied by an analysis certificate. Neither of these should be accepted as correct until a competent member of the dive team has analysed at least the oxygen content. This analysis should be conducted on delivery and immediately before use of the gas.

Saturation diving

Lost closed bell contingency plan

66[*] A contingency plan should exist for the relocation and recovery of a lost closed bell. This should identify the role of the diving contractor and other personnel, and the provision of specific equipment such as locators.

6(2), 8(1),(3)

[*] See Annex 5 for relevant technical guidance

Hyperbaric evacuation

67   In an emergency, divers in saturation cannot be evacuated by the same methods as other crew members. Special arrangements and procedures should be made to evacuate them safely while keeping them under pressure, for example in a chamber or lifeboat capable of being removed from the worksite to a safe location while maintaining life support for a minimum of 24 hours. The exact design of such equipment and its method of deployment will depend on a number of factors including the facilities available, the number of divers to be evacuated and the location of the worksite.

68   Additional safety requirements may be necessary for those personnel conducting the evacuation.

Length of diver's umbilical

69*   The length of the diver's umbilical in relation to the worksite should be included in the diving project plan, particularly where an emergency situation might require rapid location and recovery of a diver.

70*   When a diving bell is being used from a dynamically positioned vessel, fouling and snagging hazards in relation to umbilical length should also be considered.

Transfer under pressure

71*   The transfer of divers or equipment into or out of the saturation chamber, or between chambers under pressure, increases the risk of catastrophic depressurisation. Internal doors, that is those between the transfer chamber and the trunking to the diving bell and those separating living chambers within the chamber complex, should be kept closed at all times except when divers are passing through them.

Medical and physiological considerations

Liaison with a doctor

72*   The situation where a member of the dive team is injured or becomes ill but a doctor is not available at the worksite should be considered. This should include, for example, an arrangement to allow the personnel at the site to communicate by radio or telephone with the diving contractor's medical adviser, and the pre-agreement of a suitable method of transferring information from the site to a doctor.

Treatment of patients in a hyperbaric chamber

73*   A seriously ill or injured diver in a hyperbaric chamber cannot be treated in the same way as at atmospheric pressure. If the required treatment cannot be administered by the personnel at the worksite, trained medical staff and specialised equipment should be transported to the casualty. Treatment should be given to the injured diver inside the hyperbaric chamber. The diver should not be decompressed or transferred to any other location until in a stable condition.

* See Annex 5 for relevant technical guidance

Diver monitoring

74[*] Supervisors should monitor divers' breathing patterns and receive verbal reports from divers of their condition. Monitoring the temperature, heart rate or other physiological parameters of the divers does not assist the supervisor's assessment of safety.

Adjacent noisy operations

75   There are potential problems for divers and the dive team exposed to high noise levels. Noise reduction and hearing protection procedures should be used.

Seismic operations and sonar transmissions

76[*] If there is any possibility of sonar or seismic activity in the vicinity of a diving project, guidelines for the safety of the diver should be in place.

Decompression illness

77[*] Divers are at risk of DCI. It is difficult to treat DCI if access to recompression facilities is not immediately available. The diving contractor should identify the arrangements in place for the treatment of decompression illness. Divers should remain close to suitable recompression facilities for a set time following a dive.

Altitude changes

78[*] Guidance on travelling/flying after diving should be in the diving contractor's generic risk assessment. If these factors are relevant to a particular diving project they should be identified in the diving project plan.

Thermal stress

79[*] Excessive heat and cold can affect the health, safety and efficiency of divers and the dive team. Appropriate personal protective equipment and procedures should be provided to maintain thermal balance. For example, divers may be provided with suitable passive or active heating, such as thermal undergarments and a well-fitting 'dry' diving suit, or a hot-water suit. 'Wet' suits have limited application for diving within the scope of this Code.

80   Divers who breathe oxygen and helium mixtures require active heating. Their inspired breathing gas will require active heating for dives deeper than 150 metres.

Duration of saturation exposure

81   When planning a dive, consideration should be given to the previous saturation exposures of each diver and the time that he or she has spent at atmospheric pressure since completing his or her last saturation dive.

82[*] Because of the effects of long periods under pressure on the diver's health, safety and efficiency, divers should not be in saturation for a continuous period of more than 28 days under normal circumstances, including decompression.

[*] See Annex 5 for relevant technical guidance

83   Saturation diving should be planned so that each period spent in saturation by the diver is followed by a surface interval of equal duration. Shorter periods at atmospheric pressure are possible, but only in consultation with the diving contractor's hyperbaric medical adviser.

Familiarisation

84   When arriving at a dive site before the start of a project, all members of the dive team should familiarise themselves with the project, plant, and any other relevant details, for example the deck layout of a ship.

85   A familiarisation programme should be included in the diving project plan. The personnel carrying out any explanations or training should be identified and their names recorded in the diving project plan. Completion of the training by each individual in the dive team should be recorded.

86   The time required for familiarisation will depend on the experience of the individual and whether that individual has previously carried out the same job in that location. For example, a diver returning to the same offshore worksite after a period of leave may only require a few minutes to become acquainted with any changes since his or her leave; a supervisor arriving at an unfamiliar saturation diving worksite may require many hours or even days to become familiar with the site.

Use of checklists

87   A diving project will involve sequences, some of which may be complex, of different steps. There is a risk that steps may be omitted or taken out of sequence. A suitable way to ensure the thoroughness of such sequences is the use of prepared checklists that require relevant personnel to tick a box to demonstrate correct completion. Diving contractors should ensure that such checklists are prepared, authorised and used as part of the management systems for diving projects. Their use should be recorded in a suitable format.

Dive teams and associated working practice

(3)   The diving contractor shall -

(a)   ensure that there are sufficient people with suitable competence to carry out safely and without risk to health both the diving project and any action (including the giving of first-aid) which may be necessary in the event of a reasonably foreseeable emergency connected with the diving project;

ACOP

Dive teams

88[*]   The diving contractor must specify the minimum size of the dive team based on the details of the diving project and the risk assessment. There must be a sufficient number of competent and, where appropriate, qualified personnel to operate all the diving plant and to provide support functions to the dive team. This may require additional deck support personnel and other management or associated technical support personnel, for example project engineers or vessel maintenance technicians.

89   The diving contractor and the supervisor must satisfy themselves that each diver has the competences for the specific tasks required during a particular diving operation. Previous experience of a similar task may demonstrate competence but care should be taken that the diver's true experience is established beyond reasonable doubt. On-the-job or other training may be necessary for individuals to gain competence. When an inexperienced diver is gaining experience in a dive team the other team members and the supervisor should be aware of this and provide support.

Overall management

90   The diving contractor should provide a clear reporting and responsibility structure in the diving project plan which takes into account that certain individuals, for example supervisors, have specific responsibilities that cannot be changed.

91   On projects where more than one supervisor is required, dedicated personnel may be needed to provide safe management control. These personnel are often called senior supervisors or superintendents, and may or may not perform 'hands-on' duties as part of the dive team.

Dive team size

92   The required size of the dive team will depend on the risk assessment which should take into account the number of hours to be worked each day, the type of diving, the diving apparatus and the techniques to be used, any decompression requirements, the surface and underwater plant and safe systems of work being used, and the appropriate number required for safety.

Surface-supply

93   The minimum team size normally required to conduct a surface-

[*] See Annex 5 for relevant technical guidance

supply dive safely within the scope of this Code is five - a supervisor, a working diver, a standby diver, a tender (see paragraph 98) for the working diver and a tender for the standby diver. Additional personnel may be required to operate or maintain specialised plant, for example winches, and to assist in an emergency.

Closed bell

94   A closed bell project normally requires at a minimum two operations: the first when the divers are in the bell or in the water under the control of a diving supervisor; and a second under the control of a life-support supervisor when the divers are in the saturation chambers. The minimum team size normally required is nine - a diving supervisor, a relief diving supervisor, a life-support supervisor, a life-support technician, two divers inside the bell, a diver on the surface, a tender for the surface diver and an equipment technician.

95   During closed bell diving operations two members of the on-shift team should be competent to supervise. One of these persons should be the diving supervisor for the operation and the other should be in, or in the vicinity of, the dive control and able to provide assistance or relief as required. In agreement with the supervisor, the relief supervisor may take short (30 minutes) meal/comfort breaks. Any changeover of supervisor should be noted in the diving operation record and the relevant people notified, for example the divers and deck crew.

96[*]   Divers in saturation should be given at least 12 continuous hours of rest in each 24-hour period. To prevent 'ratcheting', divers should normally only take part in one bell run routine of no more than 8 hours in any 24-hour period.

97[*]   Bell runs should not exceed 8 hours from 'lock-off' to 'lock-on':

(a)   in a two-person bell each diver should spend no more than 4 hours out of the bell in the water;

(b)   in a three-person bell two divers may 'lock-out' together. The third person will undertake the duties of bellman and should remain dry unless called upon to 'lock-out' in an emergency. Each diver may spend up to 6 hours out of the bell in the water so long as an adequate refreshment break is offered within 3 hours of the start of the 'lock-out'.

Tenders

98   The diving contractor must establish the competence of a tender. The tender should be familiar with the diving procedures to be used and the contingency and emergency plans for the project.

99   For umbilicals or lifelines that are tended from the surface, at least one tender is required for each diver in the water. For umbilicals tended from a basket or stage, one tender is required for every two divers in the water. In depths of less than 50 metres, a tender may not be required if an effective mechanical handling system for the umbilical is fitted to the bell or basket.

* See Annex 5 for relevant technical guidance

Standby diver

100 A standby diver should be in immediate readiness to provide any necessary assistance to the diver, whenever the diver is in the water. There should be one standby diver for every two divers in the water.

101 The standby diver should be dressed to enter the water, but does not have to wear a mask or helmet. This equipment should, however, be immediately to hand.

102 For surface-supplied diving, the standby diver should remain on the surface.

103 When using a standby diver from a closed bell, the standby diver should remain inside the bell. Another diver should be on the surface with equipment suitable for intervention within the surface diving range. This diver does not have to be dressed for diving provided that the equipment is readily available, and may undertake duties within the dive team while the bell is under water.

Life-support personnel

104 Competent and qualified life-support personnel are needed to look after divers living in saturation. When divers are in saturation, at least one life-support person should be present at, and at least one other life-support person in the vicinity of, the life-support control point at all times.

105 A separate life-support supervisor must be appointed in writing by the diving contractor if the life-support control is remote from the diving control. Saturation diving supervisors are qualified to act as life-support supervisors.

Overlapping functions

106 Individuals in a dive team may carry out more than one duty, provided that they are qualified and/or competent to do so and that their different duties do not interfere with each other or affect the safety of the dive team. For example, divers may carry out other associated duties while waiting to dive, such as acting as tenders or standby divers, or operating and attending to plant.

Surface compression chambers

107 The controls of a surface compression chamber should only be operated by persons competent to do so. Such competence will be achieved by a combination of training and experience. The training of divers and life-support technicians for the offshore sector will have covered the operation of such chambers. The degree of supervision provided should reflect the experience of the operator.

108 Supervisors may exercise full control over the operation of a surface compression chamber provided that they are able to clearly see and hear what is happening either directly or by video and audio links. If the supervisor cannot exercise this level of control, responsibility for that part of the diving project must be given to another supervisor.

Personnel not employed by the diving contractor

109 Personnel who are not employed by the diving contractor must be

carefully considered for competence and suitability before being included in the dive team. Such personnel can create a hazard if they lack familiarity with the diving contractor's procedures, rules and diving plant.

110 As an example, when a diving system forms an integral part of a vessel and the maintenance technicians are employed by the vessel owner, these personnel, whose principal duties will be associated with the diving project, may form part of the dive team. Such an arrangement should be confirmed in writing, together with the responsibilities of these individuals.

Trainees

111 While being trained for a particular role within a dive team, a trainee is not competent for that role. However, they may during that training be considered for another role in the dive team provided that they are qualified and competent for that task. For example, a diver may form part of a dive team while training as a supervisor. The trainee should not be allowed to take on the functions of the person training them unless the trainer remains in control, is present to oversee their actions, and the safety of the diving operation is not affected.

Hours of work

112 As part of the risk assessment, the effects of working time, such as fatigue, on the level of risk to which workers may be exposed should be evaluated. Fatigue is a result of prolonged mental or physical exertion. It can affect people's performance and impair their mental alertness, which could in turn endanger the safety of the dive team.

113 Factors to be taken into account include:

(a) working patterns (eg availability of rest and refreshment breaks);

(b) the nature and demands of the job;

(c) the working environment;

(d) the work activity;

(e) sleep deprivation.

114 A review of the risk assessment should be carried out when planning increases to the existing limits on hours of work, or before making any significant changes to working arrangements.

115 Measures which can control or mitigate undesirable effects on health or safety caused by fatigue include:

(a) providing adequate staffing levels and relief systems to avoid regular working of excessive hours;

(b) designing shift systems to minimise the potential for health and safety problems;

(c) ensuring all personnel receive adequate rest periods, particularly at busy times;

(d) allowing regular short breaks during shifts;

(e)   having contingency plans for unforeseen events.

116   Diving contractors should ensure that they have adequately assessed and provided for any health or safety problems that might arise.

First aid

117   Because emergency medical services are not immediately available, for diving within the scope of this Code, all divers should have an up-to-date first-aid qualification. For all diving projects under these Regulations, the required standard is the first aid at work standard, as defined by the Health and Safety (First-Aid) Regulations 1981 Approved Code of Practice.

118   The diver training programme includes training in diving physiology and medicine. The ability to use those skills and knowledge forms an integral part of the diver competence assessment. At the time of their diver training, trainees will also be taught and assessed for a separate first-aid qualification to the standard required in the Health and Safety (First-Aid) Regulations 1981. The first-aid qualification is only valid for three years. Trainees will also be trained in oxygen administration.

119   Divers covered by this Code should have satisfactorily completed a refresher course in the first-aid qualification before their certificate has run out.

120   At least one person in the dive team, other than the diver in the water, should be qualified to a diver medic standard. This person should not be the supervisor because of his or her need to be in direct control of the operation at all times. There are situations where additional members of the dive team should be qualified to a diver medic standard. This will include situations where the diver requiring first aid is inside a hyperbaric compression chamber and emergency medical assistance cannot be provided by normal emergency medical services. The diving contractor's risk assessment should consider the numbers required to be qualified to this standard.

Diving plant

(3)   The diving contractor shall -

(b)   ensure that suitable and sufficient plant is available whenever needed to carry out safely and without risk to health both the diving project and any action (including the giving of first-aid) which may be necessary in the event of a reasonably foreseeable emergency connected with the diving project;

121   The diving contractor must be satisfied that sufficient plant, suitable for the use to which it will be put, is provided for the diving project and that sufficient plant is available, whenever needed, which is suitable to carry out safely any action which may need to be taken in a reasonably foreseeable emergency.

122   Suitability can be assessed by the evaluation by a competent person, clear instructions or statements from the manufacturer or supplier, physical testing, or previous use in similar circumstances. All items of equipment worn by the diver should, wherever possible, comply with international, European or national standards.

Gases

123   Gases stored in high-pressure cylinders are hazardous. Gas storage areas should be adequately protected, for example by the provision of fire deluge systems. Gases used for diving within the scope of this Code should be handled with appropriate care.

Storage cylinders

124*   Gas cylinders should be suitable in design, fit for purpose and safe for use. Each cylinder should be tested and have appropriate certification issued by a competent person. Cylinders used for diving within the scope of this Code may be subjected to special conditions, for example being used underwater, and therefore need special care.

Marking and colour-coding of gas storage

125*   Accidents have occurred because of wrong gases or gas mixtures being used in a diving project. The diving contractor should ensure that all gas storage units comply with the international, European or national standards of colour-coding and marking of gas storage cylinders, quads and banks. Where appropriate, pipework should also be colour-coded.

Divers' breathing gas supply systems

126*   Each diver's breathing gas should be of the correct composition, temperature and flow for all foreseeable situations. This includes independent primary and secondary supplies. Gas supplies should be arranged so that interruption of supplies to one diver will not affect other divers' supplies.

127   Whatever type of breathing apparatus is in use, each diver must carry an independent reserve supply of breathing gas that can be

* See Annex 5 for relevant technical guidance

quickly switched to the breathing circuit in an emergency. This should have sufficient capacity to allow the diver to reach a place of safety.

128* An on-line oxygen analyser with a suitable alarm, for example an audible Hi-lo alarm, should be fitted to the diver's gas supply line in the dive control area, even if the breathing medium is compressed air. This will assist in preventing the diver being supplied with the wrong percentage of oxygen. In addition, a carbon dioxide analyser with a suitable alarm should be fitted in all saturation diving projects using gas reclaim plant.

Emergency breathing gas cylinders

129* When a diving basket is used by surface-supplied divers, emergency breathing gas cylinders should be supplied in the basket in a standard layout. This allows divers to access the cylinders rapidly in an emergency.

Oxygen

130* Pressurised oxygen can fuel a serious fire or cause an explosion; it must therefore be stored and handled correctly. Any gas mixture containing more than 25% oxygen by volume should be handled as if it were pure oxygen.

131* Any materials used in plant intended to carry oxygen should be cleaned of hydrocarbons to avoid explosions. Formal cleaning procedures for such plant should be provided by the diving contractor, together with written confirmation that such procedures have been followed.

Communications

132* All divers in the water require a communication system that allows direct voice contact with the supervisor on the surface. A speech processing system is required for divers who are breathing gas mixtures containing helium because it distorts speech.

133 All such communications should be recorded, and the recording kept until 48 hours after the diver has returned to the surface or the saturation living chamber. If an incident occurs during the dive, the communication record should be retained for any subsequent investigation.

Closed diving bells

134 Divers should be able to enter and leave the bell without difficulty, and it should be possible to recover an unconscious diver in an emergency. Divers should also be able to transfer under pressure from the bell to a surface compression chamber and vice versa.

135 The bell requires:

(a) doors that can be opened from either side and act as pressure seals;

(b) valves, gauges and other fittings (made of suitable materials) to indicate and control the pressure within the bell. The external pressure will also need to be indicated to both the divers in the bell and the supervisor at the surface;

* See Annex 5 for relevant technical guidance

(c)   adequate equipment, including reserve facilities, to supply an appropriate breathing mixture to divers in and working from the bell;

(d)   equipment to light and heat the bell;

(e)   adequate first-aid equipment, and lifting plant, to enable a person in the bell to lift an unconscious or injured diver into the bell;

(f)   lifting gear to lower the bell to the depth of the diving project, maintain it at that depth, and raise it to the surface, without the occurrence of excessive lateral, vertical or rotational movement.

Breathing mixture supply

136* The main umbilical system of a diving bell should be fitted with suitable protective devices that will prevent uncontrolled loss of the atmosphere inside the diving bell if any or all of the components in the umbilical are ruptured.

Emergency recovery

137* Plant and procedures should be provided to enable the diving bell to be rescued if the bell is accidentally severed from its lifting wires and supply umbilical.

138   The bell should be equipped with a relocation device using the International Maritime Organisation (IMO) agreement recognised frequency to enable rapid location if the bell is lost.

139   The bell should be capable of sustaining the lives of trapped divers for at least 24 hours.

140* The bell will require an alternative method for returning to the surface if the main lifting gear fails. If weight-shedding is employed, the weights should be designed so that the divers inside the bell can shed them. This design should ensure that the weights cannot be shed accidentally.

Emergency markings on hyperbaric rescue systems

141* In an emergency, it is possible that personnel with no specialised diving knowledge will be the first to reach a hyperbaric rescue system. To ensure that rescuers provide suitable assistance and do not accidentally compromise the safety of the occupants, an IMO standard set of markings and instructions has been agreed. Such markings should be clearly visible when the system is afloat.

Medical equipment

142* A minimum amount of medical equipment is required at a diving site to provide first aid and medical treatment for the dive team. This minimum will depend on the type of diving and what is agreed with the diving contractor's medical adviser.

143* Particular problems exist if a diver becomes seriously ill or is badly injured while under pressure. Medical care in such

* See Annex 5 for relevant technical guidance

circumstances is difficult and the diving contractor, in conjunction with the company's medical adviser, should prepare contingency plans for such situations.

Lifting plant to carry personnel

144 Particular safety standards should be applied when using lifting equipment to carry personnel, including any wires used for secondary or backup lifting. These wires should be non-rotating and have an ultimate breaking strain that is at least eight times that of the normal working load. Different ratios of breaking strain to working load may be necessary in accordance with international, European or national standards. HSE is developing further guidance on this in relation to the proposed Lifting Operations and Lifting Equipment Regulations.

Winches

145* Winches should be provided with independent primary and secondary braking systems. It is recommended for hydraulic winches that the secondary system operates automatically whenever the operating lever is returned to neutral or on loss of power. Both braking systems should be tested separately by a competent person.

146* Winches should not be fitted with a pawl and ratchet gear where the pawl has to be disengaged before lowering.

Diving baskets and open-bottom bells

147 A basket or open-bottom bell, used in support of surface-supplied diving, should be able to carry at least two divers in an uncramped position. It should be designed to prevent the diver falling out and to prevent spinning and tipping. The basket should be fitted with suitable overhead protection and handholds.

148* Secondary means of recovering the divers should be provided.

Medical and equipment locks and diving bell trunkings

149* The inadvertent release of any clamping mechanism holding together two units under internal pressure may cause fatal injury to personnel both inside and outside the units. Suitable safety devices, for example pressure indicators and interlocks, should be provided to ensure that clamps cannot be released under pressure or the system pressurised before such clamps are fully secured.

Therapeutic recompression

150 A two-person two-compartment chamber at the worksite to provide suitable therapeutic recompression treatment should be provided for all diving projects within the scope of this Code.

* See Annex 5 for relevant technical guidance

Maintenance of diving plant

(3)   The diving contractor shall -

(c)   ensure that the plant made available under sub-paragraph (b) is maintained in a safe working condition;

151* Diving plant is used under extreme conditions, including frequent immersion in salt water. It should therefore be maintained, examined and tested regularly. It should be inspected immediately before use by a competent person to ensure that it is not damaged or suffering from deterioration.

Planned maintenance system

152   The diving contractor should establish a system of planned maintenance for plant. Maintenance arrangements should take into account both passage of time and usage. Details of the maintenance arrangements should be entered in the diving project plan. The arrangements should identify the item of plant, the date of the check, any limitations as to use, any repairs or modifications carried out and the name of the competent person.

153   A plant register should be maintained at the worksite with copies of all relevant certificates of examination and tests. It should contain any relevant additional information, for example details of the materials used to construct diving bells and surface compression chambers. It should also contain any details of any design limitations for use, for example maximum weather conditions, if applicable.

Periodic examination, testing and certification

154* The frequency and extent of examination and testing required for all items of plant used in a diving project should be in accordance with relevant statutory provisions, and international, European or national standards.

Pre-dive visual inspection

155   The dive team should be asked to carry out a pre-dive visual inspection and check the plant that they are to use, to ensure that it is in serviceable condition and working.

Cylinders used under water

156* Divers' emergency gas supply cylinders and other cylinders used under water can suffer from accelerated corrosion and must be regularly examined and maintained.

Diving bell and basket lift wires

157* Frequent immersion in salt water, shock loading from waves, passing over multiple sheaves and so on can cause wear and

* See Annex 5 for relevant technical guidance

deterioration to the lift wires of diving bells and baskets if they are not properly maintained. Specialised advice on maintenance must be followed to ensure that wires remain fit for purpose.

Lift bags

158[*] Special requirements for the periodic examination, testing and certification of lift bags have been established. Manufacturers' maintenance instructions and testing requirements should be followed.

[*] See Annex 5 for relevant technical guidance

Supervisors

(1)   Only one supervisor shall be appointed to supervise a diving operation at any one time.

159   For each diving project, the diving contractor must evaluate how much of the project can be supervised safely by one person. Enough supervisors must be appointed to cover the entire diving project so that, for example, if a diving project is taking place over such an area or time-scale that it cannot be safely controlled by one supervisor, it should be divided into separate diving operations with further supervisors being appointed for every identified diving operation.

160   The supervisor must be appointed in writing by the diving contractor. When more than one supervisor is on duty at the same time the diving contractor should specify in the diving project plan the areas and duration of the project that are controlled by each supervisor. In particular, each supervisor must have immediate overriding control of all safety aspects for the diving operation for which he or she is appointed. The diving contractor may also need to provide a management structure in the diving project plan. When a supervisor hands over supervisory responsibilities to another supervisor, this should be recorded in the diving operation record.

161   During a continuous saturation diving project two supervisors should be on each shift and will therefore be able to act as relief for each other. The name of the supervisor in control should be recorded in the diving operation record with handovers for relief, or other purposes, also recorded.

(2)   No person shall be appointed, or shall act, as a supervisor unless he is competent and, where appropriate, suitably qualified to perform the functions of supervisor in respect of the diving operation which he is appointed to supervise.

Qualifications

162[*]   Industry runs a recognised certification scheme for air diving supervisors, life-support technicians and bell diving supervisors. Any person appointed as a supervisor under this Code must possess the correct certificate for the planned diving operation.

163   A supervisor should be suitably qualified for the diving techniques to be used during his or her diving operation, or have acted as a supervisor of a diving operation in which the same diving techniques were used during the two-year period before 1 July 1981. For example, a supervisor qualified to take charge of an air operation only is not qualified to take charge of a bell operation whereas a bell diving supervisor is qualified to take charge of both types of operation.

164   Supervisors do not have to have a certificate of medical fitness to dive or to be qualified in first aid. However, the diving contractor must assess the first-aid capabilities of other personnel in the dive team and the role that the supervisor would play in an emergency.

* See Annex 5 for relevant technical guidance

30

Competence

165 The diving contractor must consider the competence of a person before appointing him or her as a supervisor. When considering competence, the diving contractor should consider questions such as whether the person is knowledgeable, practical, reliable; capable of conducting the diving operation in a safe manner; capable of managing members of the diving team appropriately; capable of acting sensibly in an emergency; and so on.

166 The diving contractor will be in a good position to decide on the person's competence if the candidate has worked for the company for some time. If the diving contractor does not know the person, it will be necessary to make appropriate enquiries concerning knowledge and experience.

Knowledge and experience

9(2)

167 The supervisor must have adequate practical and theoretical knowledge and experience of the diving techniques to be used in the diving operation for which he or she is appointed.

Regulation 10

(1)   The supervisor shall, in respect of the diving operation for which he has been appointed as supervisor -

(a)   ensure that it is carried out, so far as is reasonably practicable -

(i)   without risk to the health and safety of all those taking part in that operation and of other persons who may be affected thereby;

Responsibility of the supervisor

168 The supervisor with responsibility for the operation is the only person who can order the start of a dive. Other relevant parties, such as a ship's master or the offshore installation manager, can, however, tell the supervisor to terminate a dive for safety or operational reasons.

169 There will be times, for example during diving operations from a vessel using dynamic positioning techniques, that the supervisor must liaise closely with other personnel, such as the vessel master or the officer of the watch. In such circumstances, the supervisor should recognise that the vessel master has responsibility for the overall safety of the vessel and its occupants.

170[*] To ensure that a diving operation is carried out safely, supervisors must conduct the diving operation in accordance with the requirements of the diving project plan and the site-specific risk assessment. They should ensure that:

(a)   as far as is reasonably practicable, the diving operation that they are being asked to supervise complies with the requirements of this Code;

(b)   the proposed dive site and the water and weather conditions are suitable;

9(2) 10(1)(a)(i)

* See Annex 5 for relevant technical guidance

31

(c) the risk assessment is still current for the circumstances prevailing on the day and during the dive;

(d) they understand their own areas and levels of responsibility and who is responsible for any other relevant areas;

(e) the personnel that they are to supervise are appropriately qualified and are competent to carry out the work required of them. They should also check, as far as is reasonable, that these personnel are fit, and in possession of all necessary certificates, that is medical fitness to dive, diver's certificate and first aid;

(f) the diving project plan and arrangements for dealing with foreseeable emergencies are clearly understood by all those engaged in the diving operation. This would normally be assured by a pre-dive briefing session with all those involved and, if required, suitable training;

(g) the plant that they propose to use for any particular operation is adequate, safe, properly certified and maintained. They should ensure that the plant is adequately inspected by themselves or another competent person before its use. Such inspections should be documented, for example on a prepared checklist, and recorded in the diving operation record;

(h) the possible hazards from complex or potentially hazardous plant have been evaluated and are fully understood by all relevant parties and that, if required, training is given. This should be carried out as part of the risk assessment during the planning of the operation and should be documented. If the situation changes, the risk assessment should be re-evaluated. Supervisors should ensure that documentation on the risk assessment of the plant is available and follow any guidance contained in the documentation, for example a manufacturer's instructions;

(i) all relevant people are aware that a diving operation is to start or continue. They should also obtain any necessary permission before starting or continuing the operation;

(j) they have adequate means of communication with any personnel under their supervision. So long as they have such communication they do not need to be able to operate physically every control under their responsibility. For example, a supervisor should be able to supervise adequately the raising and lowering of a diving bell if there is a direct audio link with the winch operator, even though the winch may be located where the supervisor cannot see it or have ready access to it;

(k) proper records of the diving operation are maintained. This must include the particulars in Annex 1;

(l) they are able to see divers in the bell or the compression chamber during saturation operations;

(m) they maintain the diving operation record throughout the diving operation for which they are responsible.

Regulation 11

Regulation

11

A supervisor may, whilst supervising the diving operation in respect of which he is appointed, give such reasonable directions to any person taking part in that operation or who may affect the safety of that operation as are necessary to enable him to comply with regulation 10.

ACOP

11

171   The supervisor is entitled to give reasonable orders in relation to health and safety to any person taking part in the diving operation. These orders take precedence over any company hierarchy. These orders could include instructing unnecessary personnel to leave a control area, instructing personnel to operate plant and so on.

172   The supervisor remains in overall control when a diver inside a deck chamber requires medical treatment, whether medical personnel are present or are communicating by long distance.

Divers

Regulation
12(1)(a)

(1)   No diver shall dive in a diving project unless he -

(a)   has, subject to paragraph (2), an approved qualification which is valid for any activity he may reasonably expect to carry out while taking part in the diving project;

Regulation
14(1)

*   (1)   The Executive may approve in writing such qualification as it considers suitable for the purpose of ensuring the adequate competence of divers for the purposes of regulation 12(1)(a).*

ACOP
12(1)(a), 14(1)

Qualifications

173   All divers at work must hold an approved diving qualification suitable for the work that they intend to do. A list of current approved qualifications can be obtained from HSE.

174   Divers should have the original certificate in their possession at the site of the diving project.

175   An approved diving qualification is not required either by people who dive purely as part of their training to become qualified divers or by people providing emergency medical treatment in a chamber.

Regulation
13(1)(a)

(1)   No person shall dive in a diving project -

(a)   unless he is competent to carry out safely and without risk to health any activity he may reasonably expect to carry out while taking part in the diving project;

ACOP
13(1)(a)

Competence

176   Divers must be competent to do the work allocated to them within the diving project plan. A basic level of diving competence may be assumed from a diver who has a particular qualification, that is a relevant diver competence assessment certificate. For some tasks, such as underwater inspection, certificates issued by diver training organisations or independent bodies, such as the Certification Scheme for Weldment Inspection Personnel, will confirm a diver's competence.

177   Divers can gain knowledge of unfamiliar tasks or plant by, for example, looking at the diving project specifications, the plant to be operated, the area to be worked and any other relevant factors.

(2)   Every person engaged in a diving project shall comply with:-

(a)   any directions given to him by a supervisor under regulation 11.

178   All people in the dive team have a responsibility to co-operate with the supervisor and to follow any reasonable directions and instructions that the supervisor gives.

Regulation 12

(3)   Every diver engaged in a diving project shall -

(a)   maintain a daily record of his diving;

179   Divers' daily records (logs) must include the particulars in Annex 2.

Regulation 17

(1)   Any certificate of training and any certificate of medical fitness to dive issued, or having effect as if issued, under the Diving Operations at Work Regulations 1981[(a)] ("the 1981 Regulations") shall have effect, subject to any conditions or limitations contained in any such certificate, as if it were, as the case may be, an approved qualification or a certificate of medical fitness to dive for the purposes of these Regulations.

(a) SI 1981/399 as amended by SI 1990/996 and 1992/608

180   The main and restricted HSE part certificates issued under the Diving Operations at Work Regulations 1981 are still legally valid and do not have to be exchanged for the new certificates.

181   Transitional certificates issued under regulation 15 of the Diving Operations at Work Regulations 1981 are still legally valid.

182   Certificates issued by the Manpower Services Commission and the Training Services Agency are still legally valid, but can be exchanged for the appropriate HSE certificate.

Medical checks

Regulation 12

Regulation
12(1)(b)

ACOP

12(1)(b)

(1) No diver shall dive in a diving project unless he -

(b) has a valid certificate of medical fitness to dive.

183 All divers at work must have a valid certificate of medical fitness to dive issued by an HSE medical examiner of divers. The certificate of medical fitness to dive is a statement of the diver's fitness to perform work underwater, and is valid for as long as the doctor certifies, up to a maximum of 12 months.

184 Where an annual medical examination is carried out less than a month before the expiry of the current medical certificate to dive, the start date of the new certificate may begin from the expiry date of the current certificate.

185 Trainee divers who train while at work must hold a certificate of medical fitness to dive before they begin training. This will help potential divers to be aware of any health problems that may affect their employment prospects or long-term health, should they continue to dive. The pre-training medical examination contains the same elements as the annual medical assessment with the addition of such investigations as blood group and so on.

186 Every diver, or person who is likely to be subject to hyperbaric conditions as routine rather than in an emergency, must have a valid certificate of medical fitness to dive.

Regulation 15

Regulation
15(1)

ACOP

15(1)

(1) A certificate of medical fitness to dive is a certificate from a medical examiner of divers (or from the Executive following an appeal under paragraph (4)) that the person issuing the certificate considers the person named in the certificate to be fit to dive.

187 The medical examination and assessment look at the diver's overall fitness to dive. These include the main systems of the body - cardiovascular system, respiratory system and central nervous system - as well as the ears, nose and throat, vision, dentition, and the person's capacity for exercise.

Regulation 13

Regulation
13(1)(b)

ACOP

13(1)(b)

(1) No person shall dive in a diving project -

(b) if he knows of anything (including any illness or medical condition) which makes him unfit to dive.

188 Persons who dive in a diving project and who consider themselves unfit for any reason, for example fatigue, minor injury, recent medical treatment, must inform their supervisor. Even a minor illness, such as

ACOP

the common cold or a dental problem, can have serious effects on a diver under pressure, and should be reported to the supervisor before the start of a dive. Supervisors should seek guidance from the diving contractor or the company's medical adviser if there is doubt about that person's fitness to dive.

189[*] People who dive in a diving project and who have suffered an incident of DCI should record details of the treatment that they received in their daily record (log book). They should show this to the supervisor before taking part in their first dive after the treatment in order that a check can be made of their fitness to return to diving. Supervisors should seek guidance from the diving contractor or the company's medical adviser if there is doubt about that person's fitness to dive.

190 Before saturation exposure, the supervisor should ensure that a diver has had a medical check within the previous 24 hours. This will confirm, as far as reasonably practicable, the diver's fitness to enter saturation. The medical check will be carried out by a nurse, doctor or diver medic. The content of the medical check and the format of the written record may be decided by the diving contractor, and should be specified in the diving contractor's diving manual.

13(1)(b)

191 Before any dive not involving saturation, the supervisor should ask the divers to confirm that they are fit to dive and record this confirmation in the diving operation record.

Regulation 15

Regulation

15(6)

(6) In this regulation, "medical examiner of divers" means a medical practitioner who is, or who falls within a class of medical practitioners which is, for the time being, approved in writing by the Executive for the purposes of this regulation; and any such approval may be given generally or restricted to any class of diver or dive.

ACOP

192 HSE approves doctors to carry out diving medical examinations and assessments. These medical examiners are selected for approval based on their training in diving physiology and their knowledge of diving. This approval is for a limited period, usually for one or two years. Details are available from HSE.

15(6)

[*] See Annex 5 for relevant technical guidance

Particulars to be included in the diving operation record

1   Name and address of the diving contractor.

2   Date to which entry relates and name of the supervisor or supervisors (an entry must be completed daily by each supervisor for each diving operation).

3   Location of the diving operation, including the name of any vessel or installation from which diving is taking place.

4   Names of those taking part in the diving operation as divers and other members of the dive team.

5   Approved Code of Practice that applies to the diving operation.

6   Purpose of the diving operation.

7   Breathing apparatus and breathing mixture used by each diver in the diving operation.

8   Time at which each diver leaves atmospheric pressure and returns to atmospheric pressure plus his bottom time.

9   Maximum depth which each diver reached.

10 Decompression schedule containing details of the pressures (or depths) and the duration of time spent by divers at those pressures (or depths) during decompression.

11 Emergency support arrangements.

12 Any emergency or incident of special note which occurred during the diving operation, including details of any decompression illness and the treatment given.

13 Details of the pre-dive inspection of all plant and equipment being used in the diving operation.

14 Any defect recorded in the functioning of any plant used in the diving operation.

15 Particulars of any relevant environmental factors during the operation.

16 Any other factors likely to affect the safety or health of any persons engaged in the operation.

17 Name and signature of the supervisor completing the record.

18 Affix company stamp (if appropriate).

Details to be included in the diver's daily record (log)

Names and addresses should be printed and in block capitals.

1   Name and signature of the diver.

2   Name and address of the diving contractor.

3   Date to which entry relates.

4   Location of the diving operation, including the name of any vessel or installation from which diving is taking place.

5   The maximum depth reached on each occasion.

6   The time the diver left the surface, the bottom time, and the time the diver reached the surface on each occasion.

7   Where the dive includes time spent in a compression chamber, details of any time spent outside the chamber at a different pressure.

8   Breathing apparatus and breathing mixture used by the diver.

9   Any decompression schedules followed by the diver on each occasion.

10 Any work done by the diver on each occasion, and the plant (including any tools) used in that work.

11 Any episode of barotrauma, discomfort or injury suffered by the diver, including details of any decompression illness and the treatment given.

12 Any emergency or incident of special note which occurred during the diving operation.

13 Any other factor relevant to the diver's health or safety.

14 Name and signature of the authorised representative of the diving contractor (this will normally be the diving supervisor) who confirms the details recorded.

Glossary of terms and abbreviations

Competence

Competence means having a combination of training, knowledge and experience such that the person can do the job required in a safe and efficient manner.

Continuous saturation diving operations

Continuous saturation diving operations will exist when less than 8 hours separate the return to the living chambers of one team of divers and the departure from the living chamber of another team of divers.

Hazard

A hazard is something with the potential to cause harm. This may include water, environmental factors, plant, methods of diving and other aspects of work organisation.

Permit-to-work system

A formal written system used to control certain types of work which are identified as involving significant risk.

Risk

A risk is the possibility that someone will be harmed by an identified hazard. The extent of the risk includes the numbers of people who might be affected by the risk.

Risk assessment

A risk assessment is a careful examination of what causes harm and an evaluation of precautions that can be taken to prevent harm.

Surface-orientated diving

A diving technique in which the diver enters the water from the surface and then returns to the surface after completion of the dive, other than by means of a closed diving bell.

AODC
Association of Offshore Diving Contractors
(Superseded by ADC and IMCA from 1 April 1995)

DCI
Decompression illness

DVIS
Diving Information Sheet

DMAC
Diving Medical Advisory Committee

DP
Dynamically positioned

HSC
Health and Safety Commission

HSE
Health and Safety Executive

IMCA
International Marine Contractors Association

IMO
International Maritime Organisation

MSC
Manpower Services Commission

ROV
Remotely operated vehicle

SCUBA
Self-contained underwater breathing apparatus

TSA
Training Services Agency

Major legislation

This legislation covers all industries and may be relevant to diving projects. The list is not exhaustive.

1   *The Health and Safety at Work etc Act 1974.*

2   *Employers' Liability (Compulsory Insurance) Act 1969* requires employers to take out insurance to cover their liability for accidents and ill health sustained by their employees.

3   *Health and Safety (Display Screen Equipment) Regulations 1992* set out requirements for work with visual display units.

4   *Management of Health and Safety at Work Regulations 1999* require employers to carry out risk assessments, make arrangements to implement necessary measures, appoint competent people and arrange for appropriate information and training.

5   *Manual Handling Operations Regulations 1992* cover the moving of objects by hand or bodily force.

6   *Personal Protective Equipment Regulations 1992* require employers to provide appropriate protective clothing and equipment for their employees.

7   *Provision and Use of Work Equipment Regulations 1998* require that equipment provided for use at work including machinery is safe.

8   *The Offshore Installations and Pipelines Works (First-Aid) Regulations 1989* cover requirements for first-aid offshore.

9   *Noise at Work Regulations 1989* require employers to take action to protect employees from hearing damage. The Regulations now apply offshore.

10   *Electricity at Work Regulations 1989* require people in control of electrical systems to ensure they are safe to use and maintained in a safe condition. The Regulations now apply offshore.

11   *Health and Safety (Training for Employment) Regulations 1990* set out how certain people being trained for employment should be treated for the purposes of health and safety law.

12   *Offshore Installations (Safety Case) Regulations 1992* require the duty holder of an offshore installation to submit at various stages in the life cycle of the installation a safety case for the management of health and safety on the installation.

13   *Chemicals (Hazard Information and Packaging for Supply) (Amendment) Regulations 1998 and 1999* require suppliers to classify, label and package dangerous chemicals and provide safety data sheets for them.

14   *Construction (Design and Management) Regulations 1994* cover safe systems of work on construction sites.

15 *Control of Substances Hazardous to Health Regulations 1999* require employers to assess the risks from hazardous substances and take appropriate precautions.

16 *Health and Safety Information for Employees (Modifications and Repeals) Regulations 1995* require employers to display a poster telling employees what they need to know about health and safety.

17 *Offshore Installations and Pipelines Works (Management and Administration) Regulations 1995* require co-operation between everyone who has a contribution to make to ensuring health and safety on the offshore installation or in activities involving the installation.

18 *Offshore Installations (Prevention of Fire and Explosion, and Emergency Response) Regulations 1995* provide for the protection of persons from fire and explosion and for securing effective emergency response.

19 *Reporting of Injuries, Diseases and Dangerous Occurrences Regulations 1995* require employers to notify certain occupational injuries, diseases and dangerous events.

Sources of information

These sources of information are relevant industry technical guidance referred to in the Approved Code of Practice. This does not mean, however, that the industry guidance has the legal status of an Approved Code of Practice.

Reference	Title	Paragraph(s)
AODC 065	SCUBA	42
DVIS3	Breathing gas management (section on use of SCUBA in commercial diving)	42
DVIS5	Exposure limits for air diving operations	44
AODC 055	Protection of water intake points for diver safety	47
AODC 034	Diving when there is poor surface visibility	49
AODC 047	The effects of underwater currents on divers' performance and safety	50
AODC 032 (Rev)	Remotely operated vehicle intervention during diving operations	51
AODC 035	Code of Practice on the safe use of electricity under water	52
AODC 062	Use of battery operated equipment in hyperbaric conditions	53
AODC 054	Prevention of explosions during battery charging in relation to diving systems	53
DVIS1	General hazards (section on explosion hazards from sub-sea housings containing rechargeable batteries)	53
DMAC 03	Accidents with high pressure water jets	54
AODC 049	Code of practice for the use of high pressure water jetting equipment by divers	54
AODC 063	Underwater air lift bags	55
DVIS1	General hazards (section on abrasive cutting discs)	56
DVIS1	General hazards (section on prevention of explosions during oxy-arc cutting operations)	57
MaTR133	Investigations into the damage caused to a diver's helmet by an explosion during oxy-arc operations in the North Sea	57
IMCA 010	Diving from vessels operating in dynamically positioned mode	58

Reference	Title	Paragraph(s)
DVIS1	General hazards (section on diving from dynamically positioned vessels)	58
DPVOA 103	Guidelines for the design and operation of dynamically positioned vessels	58
MSC/Circ 645	Guidelines for vessels with dynamic positioning systems	59
AODC 014	Minimum quantities of gas required offshore	61
AODC 038	Guidance note on the use of inert gases	63
DMAC 05	Recommendation on minimum level of oxygen in helium supplied offshore	63
DMAC 04	Recommendation on partial pressure of oxygen in bail-out bottles	64
AODC 016	Guidance note on colour coding and marking of diving gas cylinders and banks	65
DVIS3	Breathing gas management (section on checking contents of breathing mixtures)	65
DVIS3	Breathing gas management (section on the marking of air and nitrox quads)	65
AODC 019	Guidance note on emergency diving bell recovery	66
AODC 020	Length of divers' umbilicals from diving bells	69
DVIS1	General hazards (section on diving from dynamically positioned vessels)	70
DVIS4	Compression chambers (section on safety procedures for diving chamber operations)	71
DVIS4	Compression chambers (section on diving safety interlocks)	71
DMAC 01	Aide-memoire for recording and transmission of medical data to shore	72
DMAC 025	Recommendations for the provision of emergency care for the seriously ill or injured diver when in saturation	73
DMAC 02	In-water diver monitoring	74
DMAC 06	The effect of sonar transmissions on commercial diving activities	76
DMAC 012	Safe diving distance from seismic surveying operations	76

Reference	Title	Paragraph(s)
AODC 061	Bell ballast release systems and buoyant ascent in offshore diving operations	140
AODC 017	Guidance note on the marking of hyperbaric rescue systems designed to float in water	141
DMAC 015 (Rev 1)	Medical equipment to be held at the site of an offshore diving operation	142
DMAC 025	Recommendations for the provision of emergency care for the seriously ill or injured diver when in saturation	142
DMAC 025	Recommendations for the provision of emergency care for the seriously ill or injured diver when in saturation	143
DVIS6	Maintenance of diving bell hoist ropes	145
DVIS2	Diving system winches (section on diving bell hydraulic winch brake systems)	145
DVIS2	Diving system winches (section on air driven winches)	146
DVIS4	Compression chambers (section on safety procedures for diving chamber operations)	148
DVIS4	Compression chambers (section on diving safety interlocks)	149
AODC 056	Code of practice on initial and periodic examination, testing and certification of diving plant and equipment	151
AODC 056	Code of practice on initial and periodic examination, testing and certification of diving plant and equipment	154
AODC 037	Periodic examination of bail-out bottles	156
AODC 056	Code of practice on initial and periodic examination, testing and certification of diving plant and equipment	157
AODC 056	Code of practice on initial and periodic examination, testing and certification of diving plant and equipment	158
AODC 063	Underwater air lift bags	158
AODC 053	AODC offshore diving supervisor and life support technician schemes	162
AODC 031	Communications with divers	170
DMAC 013 (Rev 1)	Guidance on assessing fitness to return to diving after decompression illness	189

The future availability and accuracy of the references listed in this publication cannot be guaranteed.

50

Printed and published by the Health and Safety Executive   C2   12/00